HOW TO CURE WITH
ALTERNATIVE MEDICINE
WITHOUT GOVERNMENT INTERFERENCE

MOSES DURAZO
BA, HHP, CBP

ISBN-10: 1508478538
ISBN-13: 978-1508478539

Durazo Publishing
Santa Ana, CA USA
714-824-9998

Questions, Comments or Suggestions
Email: DurazoPublishing@Gmail.com

Meet the author and his *alternative* medicine practice that prevents, improves and cures in one easy
step. Subscribe for Free:

WWW.SAVEMEMAGNETS.COM

This book is dedicated to *You*, my fellow brothers and sisters, who value freedom, coexisting, peace, and are relentless in exploring and advancing knowledge in order to contribute to the betterment of humanity despite appearing to swim against the current. May we use our United States of America Constitutional Rights to set us free!

Disclaimer

The information found within is for educational purpose only and should not be considered a substitute for legal counsel from a licensed attorney in handling your legal affairs.

CONTENTS

Glossary of Terms

Throughout this book, certain terms will be used that are familiar to those of us in the business of alternative medical practices.

However, to ensure consistency and simplicity, we offer this quick guide to terms frequently used in this book.

Allopathic Medicine

Also referred to as mainstream medicine, or conventional medicine. This refers to Western medicine or modern medicine practiced by licensed allopathic physicians throughout the world.

Alternative Medicine

For the purposes of this book, this term refers to medicine or therapies that are used outside of the boundaries of allopathic medicine.

Complementary Medicine

Complementary medicine refers to the concept of practicing conventional medicine with alternative medicine. For example, a doctor may prescribe painkillers, a traditional medication, with acupuncture, a therapy practiced outside of the scope of mainstream medicine.

Members

Patients, clients or customers of the public sector become Members of your association in the private sector upon agreeing to and signing relevant document.

Introduction

Sixty-two per cent of Americans aged 18 and over use some form of non-traditional medicine annually, according to survey conducted by the Centers for Disease Control and Prevention.

People are seeking relief of their pain, return of their energy and the strength to live life to the fullest.

These alternative treatments include acupuncture, chiropractic, biomagnetism, reflexology, alphabiotics, yoga, herbal supplements, vitamin/mineral therapy, and prayer, among many others.

Some of these medicines and treatments are combined with more conventional therapies and drugs and administered by licensed medical doctors, while others are administered by alternative health practitioners.

Either way, those who offer the alternative medicine walk a fine line of what is legally acceptable practice. They work daily in fear of persecution and the threat of being charged and jailed for their healing work.

In an attempt to protect the public from scam artists and harmful substances, the pendulum has swung out of balance to threaten the working conditions of many of those who practice the healing arts.

Responsible alternative medicine practitioners are not so foolish as to suggest that no regulation of substances or health care is needed.

But history has proven, time and again as we will show in this book, that what was considered mainstream medicine at one point in time was changed in another generation to become a prohibited practice.

Those of us who practice alternative medicine believe in the freedom for people to explore options and find what works for them. We do not believe that everything that we need to know about health care has already been written or discovered.

But the price of keeping an open mind on healing people is high.

Thousands of alternative health practitioners conduct their daily work in fear of persecution. They stand in danger of any time being charged with criminal offences. Walls stand between their medical practices and their "patients".

This book is about one way to break down that wall.

It is about how those who practice alternative medicine can protect their patients' rights to their services by forming Private Medical Membership Associations (PMMA).

Protected by the First, Fourth, Fifth, Tenth and Fourteenth Amendments to the United States Constitution and Section Two of the 1982 Canadian Charter of Rights and Freedoms, these associations throw a sort of safety wall around your practice, thus helping you to interact directly with your members.

It is about having the security and freedom to innovate and develop and grow your alternative health care business to provide the best possible solutions for those in need.

This book is written from the perspective of one who has worked with the fear of persecution and then the strength of a PMMA, and has learned how much more effective a practitioner can be in the association.

For five years I practiced Goizean Medical Biomagnetism with a nagging fear and doubt of whether or not I was crossing a legal line in my explanation of the potential health benefits. This doubt haunted my work, even though I knew from personal experience how my health had been restored using this therapy.

I know the relief I experienced after I took the appropriate legal action to protect myself from potential illegal investigations by government agencies and medical associations.

When you practice under the umbrella of the proper legal structure, fear is no longer your dominant emotion. Instead, you can turn the best of your thoughts to the healing arts you choose to practice.

I believe passionately in the right of people to have options to health care services, and now I can deliver them.

I want to help others who practice what we call "alternative medicine" to experience the same freedom as I do.

This book will help you achieve that.

Chapter 1

Why the World Needs Options for Healing

Medicine is Becoming Ineffective

At some point in your life, you likely became ill enough to be treated with antibiotics.

For years, prescribing a dose of penicillin or any of the other antibiotics to kill or inhibit the growth of a microorganism that was making you ill was considered standard mainstream medical procedure.

From early childhood into adult life, we took a two-week supply to get over ear infections, chest infections, throat infections, eye infections, bladder infections, and all manner of other conditions, even influenza in some cases.

Many, many children in the United States over time found their common maladies were no longer cured by penicillin. Alternative antibiotics were sought and prescribed. Many more ultimately also found them ineffective.

The World Health Organization Acknowledges the Failure

In April of 2014, the World Health Organization (WHO) announced that antimicrobial resistance is now present in every region of the world. This means that in every country, there have been charted scientifically determined cases of patients who have drug-resistant bacteria, viruses, fungi and parasites.

Antibiotics are no longer the wonder drug of mainstream medicine.

Dr. Keiji Fukuda, assistant director-general for health security at the WHO, said in a news release that the *"capacity to treat serious infections is becoming less all over the world."*

(http://thechart.blogs.cnn.com/2014/04/30/world-heath-organization-antibiotic-resistance-is-now-a-reality/).

The problem, he suggested, was caused by over-use or misuse or improper use of existing treatments.

What happens now?

Urgent Need for New Solutions

The upshot is that in the 21st century, there is a real possibility that in a post-antibiotic era some common infections and minor injuries might kill people.

In the United States alone, WHO estimates that two million people get antibiotic-resistant infections each year. At least 23,000 of them die because current drugs cannot stop these infections.

This problem has occurred just in the last 10 years.

At the same time, the WHO called for a global action plan that included better use of vaccines, basic hand hygiene to reduce infections (such as washing hands), reduction on non-health use of antimicrobial drugs, support of research that will lead to new and better diagnostic tests, and better surveillance to get a better overall global antimicrobial resistance.

A total of 114 countries were involved in the WHO study.

The point of telling this story is not to frighten readers, but to illustrate that health care is an ever-changing practice. What was carved in stone one day is crumpled up and thrown out with the trash the next.

Medical Understanding Evolves Over the Centuries

The history of mainstream medicine is full of practices that were all the rage one day and then turned out as sheer hocus-pocus the next. Patients are no longer "bled" to heal them. It wasn't until the 1400s that the idea that diseases could be "contagious" became main-stream, even though Hippocrates recognized tuberculosis was transmitted from person to person several centuries before the 1400s.

Ancient Greeks and Romans believed in a medical theory of "humorism," which was a system of medicine that attributed the human body's workings to four distinct bodily fluids. As late as the 19th century, many doctors based their practice on physiognomy, which was a certainty that they could determine a patient's character or personality from their outer appearance, especially their face.

Medical Evolution Requires Open Mindedness

However, this book is not about questioning the validity of most conventional medicines. Rather, it is about making the case that we need to keep an open mind about alternative methods of healing since even with the best of intentions and hundreds of scientific experiments published in peer-reviewed medical journals, sometimes we still get it wrong.

This book is about the rights of people practicing alternative medicine having the freedom to do so without fear of endless persecution from the government.

History shows that mainstream medicine sometimes goes off on the wrong track. It leads us to wonder if we can really be close-minded about alternatives to conventional treatments and therapies.

In the next chapter we will look at how members of the public are starting in greater numbers to exercise their right to seek alternative medicine, either alone or in combination with conventional treatments.

Chapter 2

Interest in Alternative Medicine is Booming

More People Seeking Alternative Therapy

Over a seven year period (from 1990 to 1997), a national survey conducted in the United States showed that the number of people using one of the many complementary or alternative therapies had increased by 33.8 per cent.

Currently, the National Center for Complementary and Alternative Medicine (NCCAM) of the National Institutes of Health (falling under the US Department of Health and Human Services) estimates that about 62 per cent of Americans used some form of alternative medicine in the past year. That figure includes prayer therapy.

Among the many alternative medicines and treatments sought are biomagnetism, alphabiotics, relaxation programs, tai chi and yoga, herbal medicines, massage, reflexology, acupuncture, chiropractic, vitamins/minerals, self-help groups, spiritual healing by others, imagery, folk remedies, specialized diets, energy healing, hypnosis, homeopathy, and biofeedback, among others.

In total, there were 629 million visits by Americans to alternative medicine practitioners that year, exceeding the total number of visits to all primary care mainstream medicine physicians.

In the process of seeking health, people also paid a lot of money. An estimated $21.2 billion was spent on alternative medicine services and more than half of that ($12.2 million) was paid for without any return from insurance companies.

There is obviously a demand for alternative medicine practitioners in United States. Those who enter this domain can reasonably expect, if the playing field was not tilted against them, to earn a reasonable return for their services.

Why People Seek Alternative Medicine

To understand our own business better, it is good to understand why this growth is happening. It is certainly not only that more people are growing skeptical about mainstream medicine.

The reality is that in many countries of the world, such as Asia and Africa in particular, people do not have access to mainstream medicine, but they can gain access to alternative and complementary medicine.

In other instances, alternative medicine is sought because it is more affordable and is delivered in a more democratic environment than a conventional doctor/patient relationship that tends to dictate what you do.

There is also the reality that many people have found alternative medicine to be much more effective, non-invasive and told their stories. It has assisted in improving their quality of life and easing their pain, and they want others to know.

To meet the demand for alternative medicine services, there are many practitioners in the business. There are about 6,000 people involved in providing acupuncture services in the United States alone. About 15 per cent of the United States population is seeing a chiropractor regularly. Add to that the 50,000 qualified massage therapists working in the US, and another 50,000 biofield practitioners and 1,000 licensed naturopathic doctors.

Unequal Legal Standing of Practitioners

And yet all of these practitioners are in essence treated with a lack of status and respect afforded others who heal.

To be labeled as an "alternative" or "complementary" practitioner is the equivalent of immediately being labeled with unequal legal standing, discrimination in licensing, accreditation, reimbursement for service and other regulatory structures.

In the next chapter, we will look at ways in which the non-conventional world of medicine is regulated and how its practitioners are treated.

Chapter 3

Great Discrepancies in Medical Regulations Evident

Unequal and Confusing Laws

Like many other businesses in the United States, alternative medicine is regulated, and this book takes no issue with the concept of that.

It is natural for government to work to protect the safety and health of its citizens.

However, what is difficult for alternative medicine practitioners is the burden to carry an unequal share of regulations and never ending compliances needed to conduct our business.

There are rules surrounding whether or not we can be licensed, whether or not we can approach patients directly and what claims we can make to them, malpractice, third-party reimbursement (insurance companies) and access to treatments.

We must deal with state laws in many areas such as licensing and marketing, but federal laws, notably the Food and Drug Administration, for legal matters.

All the laws are aimed pretty squarely against the practitioners and favor the consumers.

While it is understandable for any government to work to protect people from fraud and dangers that could threaten their lives, there is so much conflict and so many foggy areas, that many practitioners feel they will never feel secure in their practice.

They will also remain confused, because there are so many mixed messages and contradictions in laws not only from state to state but from department to department. The confusion is broadened when we look at regulations in the United States compared to other nations.

This impacts not just non-licensed practitioners of alternative care, but also licensed physicians who use alternative medicine to complement their traditional treatments.

Only one thing is very clear in the U.S.A: if you practice medicine without a license you are committing a crime. The practice of medicine includes diagnosis and treating any disease or human condition.

This affects not only the non-licensed alternative medicine practitioner, but also the licensed doctor who decides to add an alternative medicine to his or her treatment options.

That is where the clarity ends and the confusion

starts.

Discrepancies in the Law

For example, the US Internal Revenue Service allows people who have acupuncture or chiropractic medical services to claim them, but will not allow homeopathic medicines to be claimed. Yet all are alternative medicines.

Herbal medicine is considered mainstream medicine in certain European countries, but alternative medicine in the United States.

The World Health Organization has acknowledged that many countries are asking it for guidance to regulate its alternative medicine industry.

The WHO has issued a statement saying it encourages its member states to integrate alternative and conventional medicine into their national health care systems and ensure their rational use.

In 1998 they released a comprehensive report called Legal Status of Traditional Medicine and Complementary/Alternative Medicine: A Worldwide Review (http://apps.who.int/medicinedocs/en/d/Jh2943e/5.html).

The tremendous discrepancy in laws regarding alternative medicine was then visible for all to see.

Consider these realities:

In Brazil, not only are there an estimated 12,000 homeopathic physicians, but since 1980, the Brazilian Medical Association has recognized homeopathy as a legitimate medical specialty. In 1988, the Brazilian government recognized homeopathy and included it in the National Health System.

In Chile, 71 per cent of the people use some form of alternative medicine such as herbalism, spiritualism, aromatherapy, and acupuncture. Equal treatment for traditional and allopathic medicine is emphasized in national policies and both are equally regulated.

In Germany, three-fourths of allopathic doctors also use alternative medicine and acupuncture treatments are offered in 77 percent of all pain clinics. There are between 10,000 and 13,000 alternative medicine practitioners. There is no legal monopoly for allopathic doctors. Licensed non-allopathic physicians can practice medicine as well as all licensed medical practitioners but some restrictions apply pertaining to certain medical acts, including x-rays, autopsies and obstetrics.

Laws Differ Around the World

The more research done, however, the more it is clear that pretty much every country in the world has different regulations for alternative medicine practice.

When you read the WHO report in detail, you discover how widespread the discrepancies are in the regulation of our industry, and it becomes clearer still that it takes a great deal of courage to attempt to heal people through non-conventional means.

Chapter 4

Legal Confusion has Practitioners Living in Fear

All Guilty of Practicing Medicine without a License

As stated earlier, in the United States, licensing laws in each state make it clear that practicing medicine without a license is a crime.

The broad definition of practicing medicine is to diagnose and treat disease or any human condition.

This is a bit ridiculous.

If this is the definition of practicing medicine, then we are all guilty of this crime to some extent, from the mother who gives cough syrup to her sick child in the middle of the night to the grandmother who promises her chicken soup will clear up the latest bout of the flu.

And practitioners of alternative medicine, despite officially using semantics and disclaimers to prove otherwise, are also practicing medicine because in fact, their goal is treatment and prevention of human conditions.

Fear Plagues Humanity

That is why many alternative/complementary practitioners go about their work with some degree of fear. That is to the detriment of the industry. Living and working in fear, as we know, brings multidimensional limitations to everybody.

Fear on any level plagues all of humanity.

In my own case and those of other Goizean Biomagnetic practitioners, for example, fear limits us from doing three important things.

First, it stops us from advancing scientific discovery.

Dr. Goiz promised the Mexican authorities he would cease research. We also hear of doctors from the United States who go to other countries like Mexico to set up their practices to apply their revolutionary methods to avoid persecution in the US. All of this fear creates a lot of confusion, does it not?

Second, fear stops us from helping more people.

If you didn't self-censor yourself and instead spoke the truth that what you're doing can prevent, improve and potentially cure cancer, arthritis and other diseases for example, then naturally more people would give it a try.

Third, fear hinders economic growth.

How can any alternative medicine practitioner increase the number of client/customers if you can't say what you really do? You can say, *"I can help you with your health issue, but I really can't because I don't give medical advice or cure people."*

This is absurd.

It's like asking our alternative medicine practitioners to have dual personality disorder. We end up contributing to everybody's confusion, especially our own, and that's no way to live!

Living in fear is detrimental to the objective of healthcare services which is to help people overcome fear.

We do not know if we will be shut down suddenly. We must be extremely cautious in approaching our patients or in making advertising promises to them. We must tiptoe across eggshells to do the healing work we want to accomplish. Is this right or fair?

Chapter 5

What Difference does a License Make?

Licensed Practitioners

Before we look at our options for getting out from under the fog of fear and stepping into the healing sunlight, let us look at one other aspect of medical practice: the licensing question.

What can you do if you have one? What can you do if you don't?

Those of us who practice alternative and complementary medicine can be either licensed or unlicensed.

What is the difference, besides a piece of paper?

A licensed medical practitioner is someone who is licensed to practice in their field, or is certified or registered in accordance with federal, state and municipal laws and regulations. They are allowed to render their services to the public.

Examples of licensed health care occupations are

conventional physicians, dentists, nurses, midwives and psychologists.

Examples of non-conventional health care occupations that can also be licensed are acupuncturists, chiropractors and masseuses.

When the public seeks services from these licensed practitioners, they have a right to know if the person delivering the service has an up to date license.

If the person who claims to have a license does not have one, that constitutes an offence and/or that person will lose their license and face prosecution resulting in civil and/or criminal penalties.

This is a serious matter.

If you are practicing health care in a manner that does not require a license or with a license, each state has different laws.

Legal Restrictions for Unlicensed Practitioners

Citing the laws of California (law SB-577 for example) (and this is reflected in many other states), if you do not have a license they will not permit you to do any of the following things:

• Conduct surgery or any other procedure on another person that punctures the skin or harmfully invades the body,

• Administer or prescribe x-ray radiation to another person, prescribe or administer legend drugs or controlled substances to another person,

• Recommend the discontinuance of legend drugs or controlled substances prescribed by an appropriately licensed practitioner,

• Willfully diagnose and treat a physical or mental condition of any person under circumstances or conditions that cause or creates risk of great bodily harm, serious physical or mental illness, or death, set fractures, treat lacerations or abrasions through electrotherapy,

• Hold out, state, indicate, advertise or imply to a client or prospective client that he or she is a physician or surgeon.

Clearly, for alternative health practitioners to conduct their business in the public is cause for great fear of stepping over the legal line.

Public Sector by Default Increases Risks of Illegality

The reality is that by default, you are operating in the public sector because you are working with people from the public. In the case of Goizean Medical Biomagnetism, for example, its multidimensional approach addresses many health issues, so depending on your wording, you could easily cross the line of practicing medicine without proper licensing or registration.

For example, when many alternative medicine practitioners meet with people, we may tell them they have a virus, bacteria, fungus, parasites, glandular/organ dysfunctions, or even intoxication. This is diagnosis.

We may also be practicing psychology and/or psychiatry without a license because we discover emotional issues such as *depression, rage, sadness, resentment* and so on. This is diagnosing mental health issues.

Some practitioners incorporate hands-on Reiki and this would constitute practicing massage therapy without a license as well.

It's bound to happen that sooner or later someone will complain and ask to see your licensing and that's when your legal problems might begin.

What do we do? We try in vain to find "ways out" of our predicament.

Chapter 6

You can't Work behind the Wall of Disclaimers

Disclaimers will Not Protect You

S ome practitioners of alternative medicine believe that if they serve up all their therapies with disclaimers, they will stay on the right side of the law.

This is not true.

In fact, disclaimers do absolutely nothing to protect you again medical boards, law enforcement investigations and prosecutions against your medical practice.

You may protest all you want.

You may tell all of your patients in writing:

"I'm not a medical doctor. I'm not healing. I'm not curing."

But this is patently false too.

If you are not healing and curing, then what are you doing?

The hypocrisy of pretending you are not what

you are is obvious. Unofficially, the exact opposite is true. You are healing. You are curing. And you are secretly crossing that fine legal line every day.

Problems with Disclaimers

I recently read an example of a disclaimer that new therapists involved in the Medical Biomagnetism field are encouraged to follow.

I am no lawyer, but even as a layperson, I could see the problems.

I am reprinting the disclaimer here with my observations after each section in italics:

Disclaimer: Therapist John or Jane Doe has been certified to provide biomagnetic therapy by the Research Center of Medical Biomagnetism, Mexico, the Autonomous University of Chapingo, Mexico and by Dr. Isaac Goiz Durán.

Thoughts: *These Mexican entities certify they provided us with education, but they have no authority, at least not in the United States, to allow or forbid the rendering of this service.*

Disclaimer: John or Jane Doe is not a medical doctor, does not give medical diagnosis or provide medical advice or care.

Thoughts: *The same entity that provided this disclaimer to students of Biomagnetism runs an online forum that talks entirely to the contrary. The con-*

versations are about medical diagnosis, medical advice and care. That's how we're trained. What else can we speak of if not medical terms?

Disclaimer: Most people need three to five sessions. Sometimes more than five are needed.

Thoughts: *If Biomagnetism is complementary therapy, then why is it now being stated as needed? Why do we need something that does not heal or cure?*

Disclaimer: I have not received chemotherapy and/ or radiation therapy within a year from today and I'm not planning on getting chemotherapy and/or radiation therapy for a year from this date since it will not be advisable to have biomagnetic therapy in this situation.

Thoughts: *This sounds like medical advice to me.*

Disclaimer: After a treatment, please remember to change your toothbrush; use a new one to avoid re-infection.

Thoughts: *What infection? I thought we don't diagnose?*

Disclaimer: You may also experience a healing crisis. Because the healing crisis is accompanied by unpleasant symptoms it is often mistaken as a sickness. In reality, it is just the opposite. It is a process in which the body is overcoming ill health and becoming healthier and stronger.

Thoughts: *That also sounds like diagnosing and medical advice to me.*

I have personally met people who have seen other biomagnetic therapists before coming to me and they say: *"The other therapist told me that Biomagnetism can cure everything."*

Dr. Goiz even states that up to 98 percent of all disease can be cured, so naturally we say the same, am I right?

If you are repeating these words and continue to operate your business in the public sector, then no disclaimer in the world will protect you from the fact that you're most likely breaking federal and state laws.

Chapter 7

Step Out of the Shadows and Do Your Healing Work

Urgent Solution Necessary

I began to research options to working in fear after I became increasingly concerned that sooner or later one of my colleagues or myself practicing in the field of Goizean Medical Biomagnetism would be accused of practicing medicine without a license.

When you work in fear, it is as if you are trying to do delicate maneuvers while wearing boxing gloves. You cannot be your best; be your most innovative, and you are not growing your business to the extent that it requires for both your *"patients"* and yourself to prosper.

Now I know this can be avoided.

The reality is that both non-licensed providers of alternative care (Goizean Medical Biomagnetists, herbalists, homeopaths, iridologists, nutritionists, and spiritualists not practicing within the tenets of a specific recognized religion), and licensed complementary/alternative care providers (i.e. chiroprac-

tors, acupuncturists, massage therapists, and natu-
ropaths) who step outside of their authorized scope
of practice risk prosecution for unlicensed medical
practice.

Because the definition of practicing medicine
without a license is so broad, all of these practitioners are constantly crossing that very fine line.

So we practice in the shadow of fear.

Private Membership Medical Association is the Solution

The solution to these inherent problems of working in the public domain is to operate your alternative medical practice in the private sector. Making
that one significant move allows you to access many
legally protected liberties that you had no idea exist-
ed including the right to practice medicine without
a license.

Forming medical associations can make all the
difference in the world!

By forming Private Medical Membership Associations (PMMA), we can ensure our personal safety
as healthcare providers and guarantee our patients
their right to accessibility to our treatment.

PMMAs are defined as for profit 1st and 14th
Amendment Private Medical Associations of private
members in the private domain.

Operating as a non-profit is not practical for three

(3) reasons:

1. The founder of a non-profit association cannot control it as trustee.

2. Even though an income tax return does not need to be filed, a 25 pages plus information return must be filed.

3. All books and records must be open to the public once every three (3) years as advertised in a newspaper ad.

PMMAs also allow you to speak freely and directly to your patients about health issues, health remedies and cures. They guarantee freedom of assembly and speech. They can be granted tax exempt organization status by the United States Department of Revenue under Section 501(c) (4).

When you form a Private Membership Association, your current and future clients become contracted members of your association.

By taking that step, it limits claims that can be made against you and allows you to talk directly to your members, to send them information and offer details about the services and products you offer.

You have privacy protection as well.

I believe that the absolute best reason to form a medical membership association is to be free to educate your members about the health features of your program.

Let me be very specific here. I am not a lawyer. I am an alternative medical practitioner who has learned firsthand how well PMMAs work.

Must Practice Safe Therapies

Keep in mind as well that being in a PMMA, while allowing you reasonable protection to conduct your alternative medicine practice in peace, does not allow you to practice harmful therapies that could cause death or injury to people. If a criminal act is perceived, state and federal agencies still have the right to intervene. Nobody is above the law or can operate totally outside of it.

What it does say is that even if your medicine or therapy is controversial or not mainstream medicine, it can still allow you to practice and to communicate with your members.

Freedom to Communicate and Grow

In summary, by forming a PMMA, you embrace a life without constant fear of interference and you can use your freedom to grow your business and develop your skills further. You can have a high level of privacy in the business and financial side of your practice.

You can practice your healing therapies with considerably less chance of malpractice lawsuits and without having to dole out huge amount of money for malpractice insurance.

You can also eliminate illegal investigations.

Chapter 8

How Forming an Association Eased my Work Stress

Goizean Medical Biomagnetism Controversial History

In 1988, Dr. Isaac Goiz Duran of Mexico City made a phenomenal discovery.

He learned that the strategic placement of magnets erase pH distortions, thus leading to biochemical balance and remarkable healing including cancers without a drop of medicine.

Today his science is known as Medical Biomagnetism, the Biomagnetic Pair or Goizean Biomagnetism.

It is rapidly gaining interest and popularity among healers and patients looking for safe alternatives to allopathic medicine that has failed them.

However, Dr. Goiz' safe and natural medical science has not developed without its share of pain and controversy. It was initially met with resistance and attacks from governmental and health care agencies in Mexico.

Because of the pressure he was under, Dr. Goiz eventually transferred his intellectual property rights to the Autonomous University of Chapingo in Mexico to end all persecution against him and allow his medical discovery to be advanced.

He also felt pressured to sign a government document in Mexico agreeing to cease further research.

All of these circumstances turned out to be a blessing in disguise. He was then free to teach medical Biomagnetism to a broader audience. But even as he teaches his skills, he warns his students to *"heal and be quiet"* so as not to invite similar difficult experiences in their lives that he experienced.

Practicing in Fear is Legally Unnecessary

Now, however, for many Goizean Medical Biomagnetic therapists like myself, as well as other non-licensed alternative/complementary therapists, it is no longer necessary to practice in fear.

I have taken advantage in the United States of my right to be part of a Private Medical Membership Association. I have seen Supreme Court decisions that supported people's efforts for freedom of speech and association under the constitution and seen that upheld through the PMMAs.

Yet I know there are still many who practice alternative medicine who are unaware of the benefits of forming these associations.

That is what has prompted us to write this book to give others more information on what to do to avoid all the legal implications and harassment they may be enduring.

Chapter 9

Results of Court Challenges to PMMAs

Government Agencies have no Jurisdiction over Private Medical Practices

Moving your alternative medicine practice from the public to the private sector makes all the difference in the world to your ability to do your healing job well and freely.

Under the protection of law in the United States of America, it is possible to work in all 50 states in your alternative medicine business and in your own environment (your own home) without worry of federal, state or local authorities.

That is because these authorities have no jurisdiction in these matters over private sector companies.

This means you can freely use modalities, techniques and any special invention you want to use at your own discretion. The only way you can come under prosecution or investigation when operation as a PMMA is if you are operating in the realm of a clear and present danger of substantive evil.

If you wish to cross borders in the pursuit of your business, remember that the PMMA will cover you if you cross US state lines, but their protection and coverage does not include international travel.

The US Constitution Supports Medical Associations

While Medical Biomagnetism and other forms of alternative medicine are not explicitly defined in the US Constitution, the Supreme Court has acknowledge that certain implicit rights, such as the right of association, the right of privacy, and the right of presumed innocence, share constitutional protection in common with explicit guarantees such as freedom of speech.

Specifically, the Supreme Court has described the right to associate as inseparable from the right to free speech.

In our case, this means we can get together with others to practice and talk about Medical Biomagnetism, and that entails pathology, diagnosing and treatment.

By forming a PMMA, we create the operating framework that allows us to provide our services in the private sector with a legally binding contract that changes public patients or clients into private contract members of our medical association.

It is a Constitutional Right Not a Legal Loophole

Operating in the private sector by forming a Private Membership Medical Association is not a legal loophole. Rather it is a constitutional right and the US Supreme Court, when challenged on this, has ruled in our favor.

For example, years ago the Chiropractic Licensing Board brought a legal complaint against Alphabiotic Private Membership Medical Associations for the unauthorized practice of medicine. The court ruled in favor of Alphabiotics in the private sector.

Another example of successful defense of a PMMA is related to the US Food and Drug Administration (FDA) initiating a civil and criminal investigation against a Limited Liability Company that manufactured and distributed herbal supplements.

The FDA completely shut them down. Their attorneys told them that the FDA can close anybody down and that nothing could be done about it.

Ultimately, however, the civil and criminal investigation was terminated when this same company became a Private Membership Association. To date there has been no contact from the FDA or any other state or federal agency to that firm; again, because the federal government has no jurisdiction in the private sector.

The fact is that there are more than 70 favorable US Supreme Court cases upholding the principles

of setting up and operating First and Fourteenth
Amendment PMMAs. There are no cases that have
ruled against these associations.

Chapter 10

The Practicalities of Forming a PMMA

The Choice is Obvious

It is now clear that, whether we like it or not, alternative medicine practitioners who do business with the public and without necessary licensing may be subject to severe civil and/or criminal sanctions, including arrest and prison time.

However, you have a protected right to change your business to the private domain and openly state what services and benefits you can offer its private members.

You can heal people and do a lot of good in this world. You can grow your business and prosper. You can invest in yourself and learn more in your selected area of interest.

Or, you can keep walking through the quicksand world of disclaimers and practicing behind the shadow of fear.

It's your choice.

If you opt for the logical option of taking the steps to form a Private Medical Membership Association, there are some considerations you must think about if you take the association route.

Define Your Services Prior to Forming an Association

First, you need to know precisely what services you offer. So long as you are not practicing something evil and harmful, you can offer the world anything you like. But you must know what that is, because when you form your PMMA, the Articles of Association must clearly describe the services, products, modalities and technologies you use in your business.

In the case of Biomagnetism, for example, you state that you offer a service that helps erase potential hydrogen distortions to correct problems related to microorganisms (bacteria, virus, fungus, parasites), toxins (environmental, pharmaceutical, supplement, food), emotional (depression, anger, frustration, hatred, sadness, and so on) or dysfunctions (organs and glands) and much more.

You will be able to change your Articles of Association if you wish to add services or delete others, but it is a difficult process. For this reason, it is really practical and best to spend sufficient time to think about the full realm of your business practice before setting things up.

PMMAs are Legitimate Companies and Pay Taxes

Once you complete your Articles of Association, you may apply for a new Employee Identification Number (EIN).

There are several other questions that come to mind in the process of forming your association.

For example, how do you file your taxes?

The Private Membership Association is not a corporation. Rather, it is an unincorporated association under Common Law. However, it does file an 1120 form similar to a corporation.

It is best to engage the services of a capable certified professional accountant from the start who understands the process.

Will you still need a License?

You will still need a license if you want to bill insurance, Medicare, auto accidents or write prescriptions among many other things. However, if you are practicing a healing modality where licensing does not even exist, then it's clearly irrelevant.

How will you help your members file for insurance claims?

Remember that any person you are billing insurance for would be treated in the public space where the licensing is required, and therefore, would be open to public scrutiny. Therefore, if you are billing insurance for a person, under that clearly labeled space, even if it is under the same roof, in that case you are not working with a Member, but rather patients/clients/customers.

Important that you understand that you will need two separate and clearly marked spaces under the same roof: one for the public and one for PMMA Members.

Members of your PMA are treated in the space designated for private practice only.

Is Malpractice Insurance Necessary?

The issue also arises of whether or not you need to keep your malpractice insurance and the answer to that is that is it basically your personal choice.

Keep in mind, however, that if you choose to continue to have a public presence, you will need to follow all the rules and regulations assigned by those agencies.

If all of your business is done through the PMA, malpractice insurance may be unnecessary.

I, personally, do not carry malpractice insurance because statistics show that practitioners are more likely to be sued when insured even if the healing modality you practice is 100 percent safe.

We live in a highly litigious world.

In the past I attended a business developing class for chiropractors (licensed practitioners). Because of the nature of their modality one would think that malpractice insurance is obligatory, but it is not.

The first thing this chiropractor told his business students was to cancel their insurance immediately.

It turns out law firms will not touch a case unless the policy can pay out several thousands of dollars.

Several chiropractors in attendance spoke of being so poor immediately upon coming out of school that they couldn't afford malpractice insurance so they "gambled". Once they started making more money, they decided they would do things the "right" way, and it was at that point that they were immediately sued.

Others noticed that the moment they dropped the malpractice insurance that the lawsuits stopped. Some had said they averaged two lawsuits per year.

Let me remind you that I am not an attorney and am not giving you advice about what to do with malpractice insurance. I'm simply telling you that you would not be alone if you canceled your policy.

Chapter 11

Who can Help you Form an Association?

Form a PMMA with ProAdvocate Group

If you want expert help in forming a Private Medical Membership Association, and I agree that taking that step is an excellent idea, I would recommend Pro Advocate Group (http://www.proadvocate.org/).

Email: protection@proadvocate.org

Phone in Texas: 214-387-0821

Address: 2591 Dallas Parkway, Suite #107,

Frisco, TX, 75034

I am not an employee of this group and I do not wish to exclude some of the other excellent groups who can also help by making such a recommendation.

Rather, this recommendation comes without strings attached. I do so because I feel they are extraordinary.

They have helped hundreds of Alphabiotic practitioners with forming their PMA and they have done a remarkable job defending them.

100 Percent Success Rate

They have successfully defended the First and Fourteenth Amendment several times and have never lost a case. I think a 100 percent success rate is beyond good.

Personally, my working relationship with them has been great, and in my heart, I know you would benefit from talking to them.

I was their first Goizean Medical Biomagnetic Practitioner so if you tell them, *"I need what Moses Durazo got,"* they'll understand your needs.

They will take you through all the other intricacies of getting your association up and running, such as forming your board of trustees or directors and defining the roles of your officers.

They have also collected a lot of resource materials to help you learn how to use your PMMA to its full advantage and protect you and your family.

These same resources also help you to educate your clients how they can join you and protect themselves and their families.

Chapter 12

Bright Future for Alternative Medicine Businesses

Alternative Medicine Practices are Growing

As people seek to gain control of their own health and have it treated more democratically within the health care system, they will continue to seek alternatives.

That, combined with the effectiveness of many kinds of alternative medicine is fuelling a growth industry that can only continue to go up in the future.

According to a recent report by Global Industry Analysts, the global alternative medicine business is expected to reach close to $115 billion this year.

Around the world, about 75 percent of the people living in emerging nations currently receive some kind of alternative medical care.

The changes in the medical field have been pronounced enough that some insurance firms are making changes, adding complementary and alternative medical care to the things they cover.

Time to Step out of the Shadows

Despite this interest and growth in our industry, practitioners still face a dizzying web of conflicting regulations and are not free to conduct their businesses in peace.

More and more practitioners of alternative medicine in the future will be stepping out from behind the shadow of fear and stress and moving toward the private world of membership associations so they can continue their healing work.

Everything changes over time, and that includes the world of medicine.

It is up to us when we believe in our practice to find ways to conduct it to the best of our ability and with whatever protection we can muster.

We pose a solution that we believe is worth serious consideration.

Additional Resources

WHO launches the first global strategy on traditional and alternative medicine
http://www.who.int/mediacentre/news/releases/release38/en/

Who traditional medicine strategy 2002-2005
http://whqlibdoc.who.int/hq/2002/WHO_EDM_TRM_2002.1.pdf

National Policy on Traditional Medicine and Regulation of Herbal Medicines - Report of a WHO Global Survey - 2005
http://apps.who.int/medicinedocs/en/d/Js7916e/2.html

Medical and health practitioners' defense
http://www.proadvocate.org/

About the Author

Holistic Health Practitioner (HHP) Moses Durazo is a Certified Biomagnetic Practitioner (CBP) specializing in Goizean Medical Biomagnetism working out of Orange County, California. He is also an avid spokesperson and advocate for the alternative medicine industry in the United States and internationally.

Durazo's books include: *1. How Magnets Can Save Your Life, 2. Biomagnetism: The Mind, Body, Spirit Recalibration System, 3. How to Cure with Alternative Medicine without Government Interference, 4. Medical Magnets: Saving Lives and Millions of Dollars in Healthcare,* and *5. Magnets to the Rescue* (a youth-oriented cartoon). To obtain health magnets to conduct your personal recalibration as outlined in the second book, go to www. SaveMeMagnets.com.

The journey that took Durazo to his current career is intriguing. He began his studies by interning as a Medical Assistant at the University of California Irvine Medical Clinic. With his mission to attend medical school, he began his undergraduate studies at the University of California Santa Cruz (UCSC).

Attracted to the world of medicine and academic

research, he served as a research assistant at the Center for AIDS Prevention Studies (CAPS) at the University of California San Francisco and Children's Hospital of Los Angeles.

At UCSC he was exposed to the field of holistic healthcare which completely caused him a paradigm shift. It was by taking an acupressure class that awakened his inner-consciousness. He wanted to learn more about the safe and natural mind, body and spirit medicines our ancestors have used throughout the centuries and completed UCSC's holistic health practitioner certification program. He also graduated with a Bachelor of Arts in Language Studies.

The combination of holistic medicine and language studies expanded his way of thinking, and motivated him to travel to Europe, Asia and Latin America. As a German-language student, in 1998 he participated in a university summer-long work-abroad program in Switzerland.

This life-enhancing experience showed him that despite our cultural differences, at the very core of our existence, all people and societies have the same struggles in life, which have to do with obtaining and maintaining optimal mind, body and spiritual balance.

Years later, a summer trip to Mexico in 2008 set into motion a curiosity that led him to look deeper into Goizean Medical Biomagnetism as a specific healthcare therapy as opposed to a "blind" application of magnetic fields such as magnet therapy (bracelets, mattresses, etc.).

On his travels he met a dentist who had given up his successful practice to dedicate himself to Goizean Biomagnetism. The former dentist told Durazo of all the healing and pain reduction he had witnessed in such a short time practicing this Biomagnetic science.

When Durazo returned to the United States, he got in touch with a biomagnetic association, but he could not obtain the direction he was seeking. He wanted to study the theories of Dr. Isaac Goiz Durán. He returned to Mexico City to study with him directly, and continued to be amazed at the healing results achieved.

At one point in his life, Durazo suffered greatly from a chronic health issue and conventional and traditional medicines and therapies did not help. However, when a pair of magnets were placed on his body, he immediately – from one day to the next – experienced great relief; he found the cure to his problem. He immediately knew that pioneering this science would be his newfound mission!

As his mind expanded to the healing options in the medical biomagnetic field, he also became more aware of the multidimensional aspect of life and reacquainted himself with his interest in holistic health training. He discovered an efficient method that honors a hands-on approach and trained in the art of Quantum Alphabiotic (Spinal) Alignments.

Today Durazo does his best to stay up to date with medical technology in order to deliver the very best in natural medical care. He discovered a powerful PEMF medical technology called the BEMER (Bio Electro Magnetic Energy Regulation), which members have been benefiting from greatly, and purchasing for their own home care.

For more information and to order, visit this link:

http://biomagnetictherapy.bemergroup.com/en-US

Book Collection

1. *Biomagnetism: The Mind, Body, Spirit Recalibration System.* This is an illustrated do-it-yourself biomagnetic system that will show you safe, powerful and effective steps to help you be in greater control of your life. Magnets are necessary and kits do exist.

2. *How Magnets Saved My Life – A Holistic Guide to Optimal Health.* If you are interested in natural ways of taking care of yourself, this book will teach you how to identify multidimensional conflicts that affect life. You will also learn how to avoid those obstacles through simple strategies at your reach.

3. *How you can Prevent, Improve and Cure Disease Using Magnets – Goizean Medical Biomagnetism and Bioenergetics: Frequently Asked Questions.* Learn in more depth how the powerful Medical Biomagnetic Pair therapy can help you and your family.

4. *Medical Magnets: Saving Lives and Millions of Dollars in Healthcare.* If you would like your medical insurance to pay for Biomagnetism, or if you work in the insurance industry and want your company to save thousands of dollars and improve patient's benefits, read this book.

5. *How to Cure with Alternative Medicine without Government Interference.* If you practice alternative medicine with a degree of fear and would like legal protection, this book is for you.

6. *Magnets to the Rescue: A Family Wellness Adventure.* This story is an adventurous biomagnetic healing cartoon for youth.

Titles also available in Spanish

Bonus Self-care Strategy: Three Magnets for Pain Relief

As a bonus to this book and insight into, *Biomagnetism: The Mind, Body, Spirit Recalibration System*, here is a highly effective pain/tumor relief protocol. It is one of several to be featured in that book.

To secure health magnets to conduct this pain relief biomagnetic protocol on yourself, you can go to www.SaveMeMagnets.com.

The following biomagnetic strategy has helped many of my clients relieve and even eliminate pain. This is a *safe* and *natural* alternative to addictive and potentially harmful painkillers.

Important notice: Some who have used this pain-relief protocol reported a *temporary* increase in pain; this is a great sign as it indicates transformation is taking place. The same people also reported that after a few minutes, the pain diminished, improved and even disappeared.

Reminder: This biomagnetic combination is not a substitute for medical care; it is for use after appropriate medical care.

My intention with this magnetic pairing is to help

you release your pain and live in peace. As you perform these magnetic pairings, ask yourself what other mind, body and spirit actions might be contributing to the pain you are experiencing.

Suggested Use:

Among the conditions and situations it is effective for are the following:

•   *Physical Trauma*: Cuts, scratches, sprains, strains, bruises, fractures, broken bones, or other. Use for 30 minutes, one (1) time per day until the pain stops.

•   *General Pain*: If the pain is a headache or stomach-ache or non-physical trauma (above), use between 1-55 minutes, up to three (3) times per day until you get pain relief.

•   *Tumors/Growths*: Use for 60 minutes, four (4) times per day, minimum 8 consecutive days and continue as needed.

3-Magnetic Combinations:

1. Place a positive magnet on the *left kidney*

2. Place a positive magnet on the *right kidney*, and

3. Place a negative magnet on the *pain-* or *growth-area*. In other words, place the negative field wherever it hurts or there is tissue growth, (i.e. head, stomach, fracture, lymph nodes tumors, and moles).(* Notice that left kidney is slightly higher than right kidney)

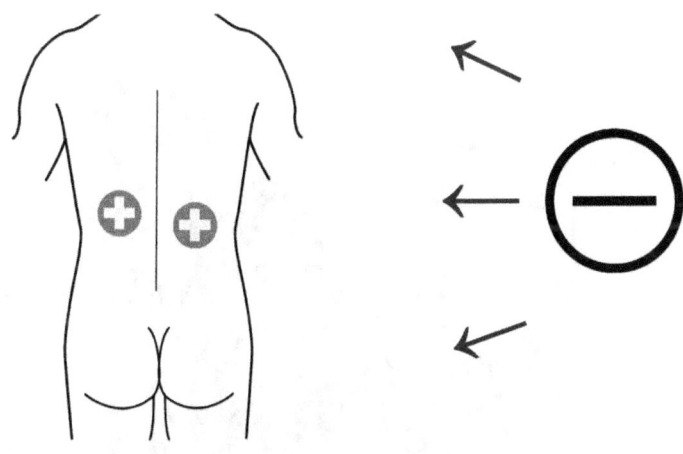

Save Me Magnets
Home-Care Kits

Learn how to use magnets for optimal wellness.
Material: ceramic permanent. **Therapeutic
Strength:** 3800 Gauss. **Dimensions:** 0.5 x 1 x 2 inches
(approximately). **Encased:** plastic for easy polarity
identification: Red/Positive (opposite side Negative).
Plastic protects against breaking and/or chipping.

Why You Need BEMER Medical Technology at Home

The BEMER PEMF medical technology is an incredible device that is helping thousands of our members at our private membership medical association to have greater healing response when combined with Biomagnetism.

Our professional and semi-professional athletes use this technology for optimal performance, as should everybody on earth.

More and more of our members are making their purchase, some of which describe this technology like being a *"doctor in a box"* - it really is that powerful and effective!

We invite you to visit our website (_www.SaveMeMagnets.com_) for more information on how you too can experience this technology for yourself.

Once you try it, we know you'll love it! We can help you order one immediately; it ships to over 40 countries.

As of October 16, 2018, you will have the opportunity to finance this medical device.

Without a doubt every family, workplace, organization, and so on, must have one in order to live an optimal quality of life.

Together we can end pain and suffering, and say hello to optimal wellness and great energy!

To order and for more information go here:

http://biomagnetictherapy.bemergroup.com/en-US